ARIZONA
DIAMONDBACKS

STARS, STATS, HISTORY, AND MORE!
BY JIM GIGLIOTTI

The Child's World®
childsworld.com

Published by The Child's World®
1980 Lookout Drive • Mankato, MN 56003-1705
800-599-READ • www.childsworld.com

ISBN 9781503828148
LCCN 2018944826

Printed in the United States of America
PAO2392

Photo Credits:
Cover: Joe Robbins (2).
Interior: AP Images: Matt York 10, Joe Caravetta 17;
Dreamstime.com: Derrick Neal 14, Jerry Coli 29;
Newscom: David Seelig/Icon SMI 9, Juan deLeon/Icon
SMI 19, Adam Bowl/Icon SMI 20, Art Foxall/UPI 23;
Joe Robbins: 5, 6, 24; Shutterstock: Tom Roberts 13,
Debby Wong 27.

About the Author

Jim Gigliotti has worked for the University of Southern California's athletic department, the Los Angeles Dodgers, and the National Football League. He is now an author who has written more than 80 books, mostly for young readers, on a variety of topics.

On the Cover

Main photo: All-Star first baseman Paul Goldschmidt
Inset: Hall of Fame pitcher Randy Johnson.

CONTENTS

GO, DIAMONDBACKS!

The Diamondbacks are the youngest team in the National League (NL). They began playing in 1998. (The Tampa Bay Rays began playing in the American League in 1998, too.) The Diamondbacks got really good, really fast! They won the **World Series** title in their fourth season. They haven't been back to the top since. But the team's fans expect that to change soon! The team has a lot of great young players and key **veterans**.

Hard-throwing Patrick Corbin is the Diamondbacks ace pitcher. ➤

WHO ARE THE DIAMONDBACKS?

The Diamondbacks play in the National League. That group is part of Major League Baseball (MLB). MLB also includes the American League (AL). There are 30 teams in MLB. The winner of the NL plays the winner of the AL in the World Series. Arizona won the World Series in 2001. The team has finished in first place in the NL West Division standings five times.

◄ *Outfielder David Peralta is part of a good group of young Arizona stars.*

WHERE THEY CAME FROM

For years, many teams got ready for the season by training in the spring in Arizona. The state never had its own big-league team, though. In 1998, MLB decided to grow. The Diamondbacks began as an **expansion** team. That means they were a new team that started from scratch. The Diamondbacks are named after a desert snake. The team is often called D-backs for short.

Steve Finley played six seasons for Arizona.
He was a great defensive outfielder.

WHO THEY PLAY

The D-backs play in the NL West Division. The other teams in the NL West are the Colorado Rockies, the Los Angeles Dodgers, the San Diego Padres, and the San Francisco Giants. The D-backs play more games against their division **rivals** than against other teams. In all, the D-backs play 162 games each season. They play 81 games at home and 81 on the road.

 Arizona players cheered as Nick Ahmed scored the winning run to beat the Dodgers in 2018.

11

WHERE THEY PLAY

It gets hot in the desert. Really hot!
So Arizona's Chase Field in Phoenix has a roof.
Chase Field is the D-backs' home stadium.
The roof can be opened or closed during a game. It all depends on the weather. If it's still too hot inside, a few lucky fans can take a dip in the pool. That's right—the stadium has a swimming pool! It is just beyond the fence in right field.

The large white panels on the roof can slide over ➤
Chase Field to protect fans from the heat.

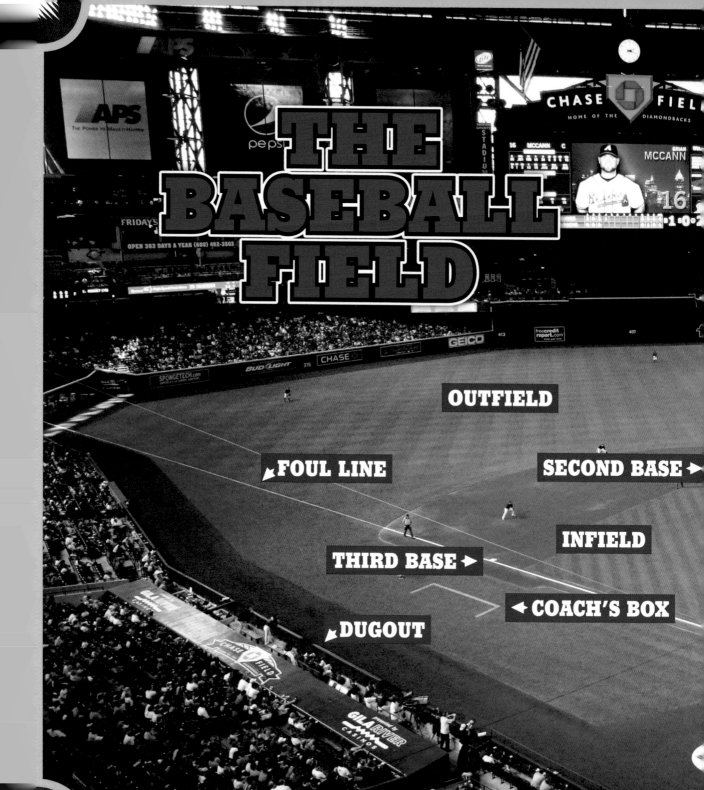

THE BASEBALL FIELD

OUTFIELD

FOUL LINE

SECOND BASE ►

INFIELD

THIRD BASE ►

◄ COACH'S BOX

DUGOUT

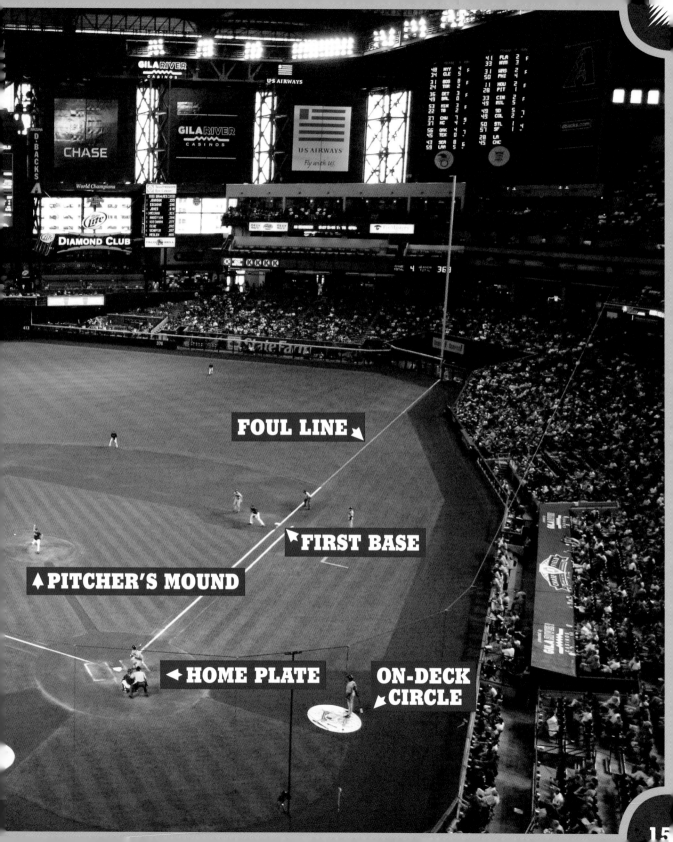

FOUL LINE

FIRST BASE

PITCHER'S MOUND

HOME PLATE

ON-DECK CIRCLE

BIG DAYS

The D-backs' greatest moment? That one is easy! Luis Gonzalez had it against the New York Yankees in 2001. His ninth-inning single won the game . . . and the World Series. Here are a few other great days in team history.

1999—The D-backs became the first MLB team to reach the **playoffs** in just their second season. They beat the Giants 11–3 on September 24. Arizona finished the year with 100 wins.

Arizona players crowded around Luis Gonzalez after ➤
his hit made them the 2001 World Series champs.

2004—Atlanta Braves hitters didn't stand a chance against Arizona's Randy Johnson. All 27 Braves batters made an out. None of them reached base. It was a perfect game! Johnson struck out 13. At 40, he was the oldest player to pitch a perfect game.

2017—The D-backs played Colorado in a wild-card playoff. Paul Goldschmidt hit a three-run home run in the first inning. Arizona was on its way to the next round. The D-backs won 11–8.

TOUGH DAYS

The D-backs haven't been around very long. They have still had a few times that their fans would rather forget.

1999—The D-backs' first trip to the playoffs ended with a tough loss. New York Mets catcher Todd Pratt was not a great hitter. But he hit a **walk-off** home run to send the Mets to the World Series.

2004—There were a lot of tough days this season. The D-backs won only 51 games out of 162. They were at rock bottom! By 2007, though, they were back in the playoffs.

▲ *Cliff Pennington was mad after he missed the ball during a big loss to Houston in 2015.*

2015—The Houston Astros were headed to the World Series this year. They stepped over the D-backs on the way. Houston scored early and often in a game played in Arizona. The Astros won 21–5.

MEET THE FANS!

The D-backs have been a big hit with their fans. Their first season, they drew 3.6 million fans to their games! Attendance has been more than two million every season since. D-backs fans are entertained by a costumed bobcat. Why a bobcat? Because Chase Field originally was called Bank One Ballpark. Because of its **initials**, the stadium was nicknamed "The Bob."

◄ *The bobcat mascot is named "D. Baxter." Can you figure out why?*

HEROES THEN

The 2001 champion D-backs had two great pitchers. Lefty Randy Johnson was one of the hardest throwers in MLB history. He could top 100 miles per hour! Right-handed pitcher Curt Schilling led the NL in wins with 22. Luis Gonzalez was an All-Star outfielder. He hit an amazing 57 home runs in the D-backs' World Series year!

With Arizona, Randy Johnson was named ➤
the top pitcher in the NL four times!

HEROES NOW

Paul Goldschmidt is the D-backs star first baseman. He hits long home runs. When he does, the team's TV announcer yells "Goldy, Goldy . . . gone!" Goldy does more than just hit home runs. He hits for a high batting average, too. He also runs well and fields well. He does it all. Outfielder A.J. Pollock is another **all-around** hero for the team. On the mound, Patrick Corbin is an All-Star pitcher.

◄ *Slugging first baseman Paul Goldschmidt is Arizona's top star.*

GEARING UP

Baseball players wear team uniforms. On defense, they wear leather gloves to catch the ball. As batters, they wear hard helmets. This protects them from pitches. Batters hit the ball with long wood bats. Each player chooses his own size of bat. Catchers have the toughest job. They wear a lot of protection.

THE BASEBALL

The outside of the Major League baseball is made from cow leather. Two leather pieces shaped like 8s are stitched together. There are 108 stitches of red thread. These stitches help players grip the ball. Inside, the ball has a small center of cork and rubber. Hundreds of feet of yarn are tightly wound around this center.

CATCHER'S MASK
AND HELMET ➤

CHEST
PROTECTOR ➤

◄ WRIST BANDS

◄ CATCHER'S
MITT

◄ SHIN GUARDS

CATCHER'S GEAR

TEAM STATS

H ere are some of the all-time career records for the Arizona Diamondbacks. All of these stats are through the 2018 regular season.

HOME RUNS

Luis Gonzalez	224
Paul Goldschmidt	209

STRIKEOUTS

Randy Johnson	2,077
Brandon Webb	1,065

BATTING AVERAGE

Luis Gonzalez	.298
Paul Goldschmidt	.297

STOLEN BASES

Tony Womack	182
Paul Goldschmidt	124

WINS

Randy Johnson	118
Brandon Webb	87

SAVES

Jose Valverde	98
J.J. Putz	83

Luis Gonzalez played in five All-Star Games while with Arizona. ➤

RBI	
Luis Gonzalez	774
Paul Goldschmidt	710

GLOSSARY

all-around (AWL-uh-ROWND) good at many different things

expansion (ek-SPAN-shun) in baseball, describing a team that is added to the AL or NL

initials (ih-NISH-uhls) the first letters

playoffs (PLAY-offs) games played between top teams to determine who moves ahead

rivals (RYE-vuhls) two people or groups competing for the same thing

veterans (VETT-uh-runs) players who have several years of experience

walk-off (WAWK-off) in baseball, a play that immediately results in the winning run

World Series (WURLD SEER-eez) the championship of Major League Baseball, played between the winners of the AL and NL

FIND OUT MORE

IN THE LIBRARY

Jacobs, Greg. *The Everything Kids' Baseball Book: Tenth Edition*. New York, NY: Adams Media/Everything Books, 2018.

Sandler, Michael. *Randy Johnson and the Arizona Diamondbacks: 2001 World Series (World Series Superstars)*. New York: Bearport Publishing Company, 2008.

Stewart, Mark. *The Arizona Diamondbacks*. Chicago: Norwood House, 2012.

ON THE WEB

Visit our website for links about the Arizona Diamondbacks:
childsworld.com/links

Note to Parents, Teachers, and Librarians: We routinely verify our Web links to make sure they are safe and active sites. So encourage your readers to check them out!

INDEX